5/09

Learning About Life Cycles

The Life Cycle of an
Apple

Ruth Thomson

PowerKiDS
press
New York

Published in 2009 by The Rosen Publishing Group Inc.
29 East 21st Street, New York, NY 10010

First Edition

Editor: Victoria Brooker
Designer: Simon Morse
Consultant: Michael Scott OBE, B.Sc

Library of Congress Cataloging-in-Publication Data

Thomson, Ruth, 1949-
  The life cycle of an apple / Ruth Thomson. — 1st ed.
     p. cm. — (Learning about life cycles)
  Includes index.
  ISBN 978-1-4358-2836-0 (library binding)
  ISBN 978-1-4358-2886-5 (paperback)
  ISBN 978-1-4358-2892-6 (6-pack)
  1. Apples—Life cycles—Juvenile literature. I. Title. II.
  Series: Thomson, Ruth, 1949- Learning about life cycles
  (PowerKids Press)
  SB363.T545 2009
  634'.11—dc22
                                       2008025778

Manufactured in China

Photographs: 8 Mark Boulton
Photography/Alamy; Cover (br),
20 Elizabeth Czitronyi/Alamy; Cover (main) Phil
Degginger/Alamy; Cover (tr), 9, 10, 23 (tl) Holt
Studios International Ltd/Nigel Cattin/Alamy; 14
isifa Image Service s.r.o./Alamy; 3, 4, 5, 6, 7, 11,
12, 13, 15, 16, 17, 18, 19, 21, 22 naturepl.com

Web Sites

Due to the changing nature of
Internet links, PowerKids Press has
developed an online list of Web sites
related to the subject of this book.
This site is updated regularly.
Please use this link to access this list:
www.powerkidslinks.com/lalc/apple

Contents

Apples grow here 4

What is an apple? 6

Apple trees 8

Buds 10

Flowers 12

Pollination 14

Apples 16

Ripe and ready 18

Fall and winter 20

Spring 22

Apple life cycle 23

Glossary and
    Further Information 24

Index 24

Apples grow here

Apples grow on apple trees. Sometimes you can see apple trees in yards. Farmers plant trees in rows in grassy fields. These are called orchards.

What is an apple?

Apples are a delicious **fruit**. They can be red, green, brown, or yellow. They can taste crisp, soft, sweet, tangy, juicy, or dry.

Apples have a thin skin
and a fleshy inside.
The **core** in the center
has dark **seeds** called pips.

stalk (which was
attached to a twig)

core

flesh

pip (seed)

skin

7

Apple trees

Apple farmers look after their trees to make sure they get lots of healthy **fruit**.

In the winter, they cut back some of the branches. This helps the tree to grow well. It also helps light to reach the leaves and fruit.

Buds

In the spring, new flowers and leaves appear. At first, they are tightly closed. They are called **buds**. Slowly, they open up.

May

On the end of each leafy
twig are pink flower buds.
When the tree is covered
with leaves, these buds
open into flowers
called blossom.

Flowers

The blossom has white and pink petals and a sweet smell. It also has a sweet liquid called **nectar** and a yellow powder called **pollen**.

petal

pollen

The scent of the blossom attracts bees to the flowers. They come to feed on the sweet nectar.

Pollination

Pollen sticks to the bee when it feeds on **nectar**.

July

When the bee flies to another flower, pollen from the first flower rubs off onto the next one. This is called pollination.

Apples

When a flower is pollinated, **seeds** grow inside it. The flower is no longer needed, so its petals drop off.

A tiny apple starts swelling around the seeds. It grows bigger and bigger all summer.

August

17

Ripe and ready

By the fall, the apples are sweeter and more colorful. They are **ripe** and ready to eat.

September

he apple tree is ready for icking. Sometimes, the ranches are so heavy with pples, they bend all the ay down to the ground.

19

Fall and winter

As the days get shorter and colder,
the leaves change color.
Soon, they fall off the tree.

November

The tree rests with its branches
bare, all winter long. New **buds**
appear on every twig.

May

Spring

In the spring, the weather warms up again. Leaves and then blossom appear. By the summer, new apples will start growing.

Apple life cycle

Buds
In the spring, **buds** swell and leaves appear.

Flowers
When the tree is covered with leaves, blossom appears.

Fruit
Apples are **ripe** and ready for picking.

Seeds
Seeds grow in pollinated flowers. Tiny apples start growing.

Glossary and Further Information

bud part of a tree from which leaves or flowers develop

core center part of an apple

fruit part of a flowering plant that holds its seeds

nectar sweet liquid inside many flowers that attracts insects

pollen grains of powder in flowers needed to make new seeds

ripe when the apple is sweet and ready to eat

seed part of a plant that grows into a new plant

Books

The Life Cycle of a Tree
by Bobbie Kalman
(Crabtree Publishing, 2002)

The Life Cycle of an Apple Tree
by Linda Tagliaferro
(Pebble Plus, 2007)

Index

bees 13, 14–15
blossom 11, 12–13, 22
branches 9, 19
buds 10, 11, 21, 23

core 7

flowers 10–11, 12–13, 16, 23

leaves 10–11, 21, 22, 23

nectar 12, 13–14

orchard 4

petals 12, 16
pips 7
pollen 12, 14–15
pollination 14, 15

seeds 7, 17, 23
spring 10, 22

trees 4, 8, 9, 19, 20, 21, 22
twigs 11

winter 9, 21